Judge Judy Adult Coloring Book

TV Icon Judge Judy Sheindlin and Reality Show, Crimes and Comedy Drama Inspired Adult Coloring Book

Cayla Preston

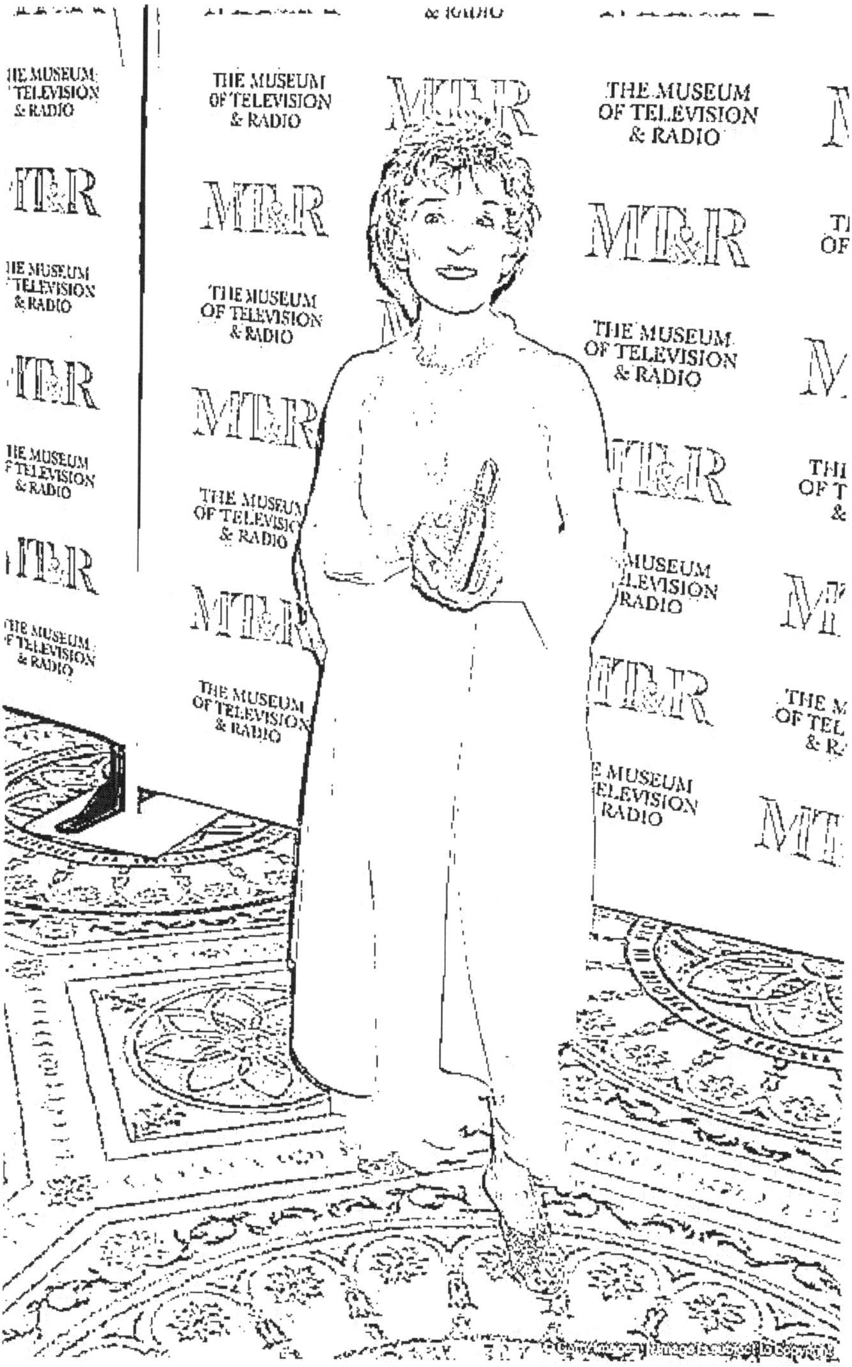
THE MUSEUM
OF TELEVISION
& RADIO
MT&R

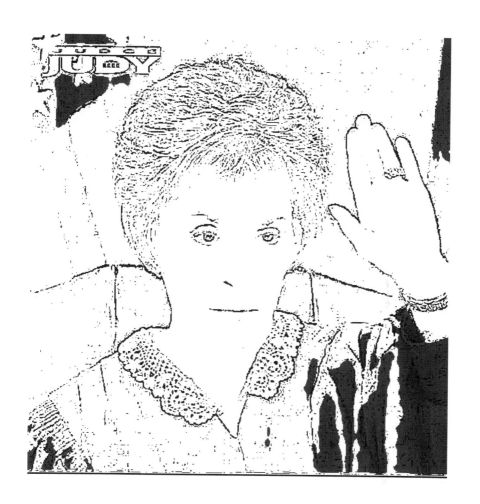

Don't try and teach a
pig to sing, it doesn't
work and only
annoys the pig.

JUDGE
JUDY SHEINDLIN

JUDGE
JUDY SHEINDLIN

14446687R00022

Made in the USA
Lexington, KY
07 November 2018